A New True Book

THE DELAWARE

By Jay Miller

CHILDRENS PRESS®
CHICAGO

Two Delaware girls dressed
in their traditional clothing

Project Editor: Fran Dyra
Design: Margrit Fiddle

Library of Congress Cataloging-in-Publication Data

Miller, Jay, 1947-
    The Delaware / by Jay Miller.
        p.   cm.–(A New true book)
    Includes index.
    ISBN 0-516-01053-0
    1.   Delaware Indians–History–Juvenile literature.
2.   Delaware Indians–Social life and customs–Juvenile
literature. [1.   Delaware Indians.   2.   Indians of North
America.]   I.   Title.
E99.D2M55   1994
973'.04973–dc20   93-36670
                                                        CIP
                                                        AC

PHOTO CREDITS

Lowanda Abraham–44 (right), 45 (bottom right)

The Bettmann Archive–35, 37

Brenda Hutchens–45 (left)

© John T. Kraft–7, 8 (bottom), 12, 15

North Wind Picture Archives–25 (right), 27, 39, 40

Archives & Manuscripts Division of the Oklahoma
Historical Society–18–#16018 Robbins Coll.
19344.4.14, 20 (right)–#16016 Robbins Coll.
19344.4.12, 20 (left)–#76103 Robbins Coll.
cd.20#11, 23 (left)–#20516.1.45, 23 (right)–
#20516.1.44 McKenney Hall 1837 litho after a 1735
painting by Gustavus Hesselius, 28–Photo by W.S.
Prettyman

Alexis Nicole Parton–44 (left)

Kristen and Mary Ann Skinner–45 (bottom right)

Tom Stack & Associates–© Don and Esther Phillips
17 (top right)

Londa and Mark Stephen–45 (top right)

SuperStock International, Inc.–© John Warden, 17
(left); © Art McWhirter, 17 (top right)

Valan–© Phillip Norton, Cover, 5, 30; © V. Whelan, 8
(top left); © Wouterloot-Gregoire, 8 (top right);
© Wayne Lankinen, 9 (left); © Roman Jaskolski, 9
(right); © Michel Bourque, 10 (left); © Stephen J.
Krasemann, 10 (top right); © J.A. Wilkinson, 10
(bottom right)

Mary Louise Watters–2, 33 (2 photos)

Western History Collections, University of
Oklahoma–Cover inset, 25 (left), 42 (2 photos), 43
(2 photos)

Tom Dunnington–Map on page 5

COVER: The Delaware River
              Inset: Reverend Charles Journeycake,
              last chief of the Delaware

TABLE OF CONTENTS

THE DELAWARE NATION

The Delaware were a nation of many tribes. They once lived along the great river between New Jersey and Pennsylvania that was later named for them. Their homes stood on the banks of the Delaware River and its branches, and along the shore of the Atlantic Ocean nearby.

The Delaware River flows between Pennsylvania and New Jersey.

Delaware families often
traveled back and forth
between the river and the
ocean.

Delaware was the name that the English gave to this nation, but they have always called themselves the *Lenape*.

Within the Delaware nation, many dialects, or varieties, of the Algonquian language were spoken. Two of the most important were *Munsi* (MUN • see), spoken in the north, and *Unami* (you • NAM • ee), spoken in the south. A different dialect was probably spoken along the coast.

Preserving fish for the winter

SEASONS

Each spring, everyone
gathered along the river to
catch fish and dry them
for the winter. In summer
months, the women grew

7

Delaware working in their gardens, where they raised
crops like pumpkins (top left) and sunflowers (top right).

corn, beans, squash,
pumpkins, and sunflowers.
In the early fall, whole
families camped in the
hills to gather fruit, berries,
and nuts. In late fall and

Bear (left) and white-tailed deer (right) were plentiful in the forests of the Delaware homeland.

winter, the men hunted deer, bear, and other game.

Children helped out year-round. They weeded gardens, climbed trees to get fruit, and ran errands for the adults.

Wild fruits such as cherries (left), raspberries (top right), and crab apples (above right) were gathered in the summer and fall.

The homeland of the Delaware was rich in many kinds of food. The Delaware people loved their land. It was a special gift to them from the Creator.

CREATION

The Delaware believed
that the Creator lived in
heaven. But he was lonely.
Below him was a giant
ocean—and nothing else.

The Creator thought
about making life. He
made a turtle that was big
enough to carry the world.
From the depths of the
ocean, the turtle rose to
the surface and floated.

The mud on its back
soon dried out and formed

11

A Delaware legend told how the world began with a cedar tree growing in the center of a turtle's back.

dirt. From this soil, a cedar tree grew in the exact center of the turtle's back. When the tree had grown tall, a man was created. He was the father of all the beings who live on the earth. Then the tip of the tree bent over and touched the earth. At that spot, a woman was created. She was the mother of all living things.

Because the turtle and the cedar tree held up the earth, the Delaware treated them with reverence. They prayed to the Creator, but also gave thanks to his helpers.

LONGHOUSES

When they were not camping, Delaware families lived in towns. Each town had several homes called longhouses. They were built with a frame of long, thin poles sunk into the ground. Their tops were tied together to make a curve. Other poles were then tied along the roof and sides. Slabs of bark

Delaware building a longhouse

were placed over the outside like shingles to keep out the rain and wind.

These houses were very long, with a door at each

end. Down the middle was
a hallway where small fires
burned every few feet.
Along the sides were
compartments where each
family lived. The families
on opposite sides of the
hallway shared fireplaces.

The clan animals of
the Delaware were the
wolf (above), the turkey (top right),
and the turtle (right).

CLANS

Every Delaware belonged
to one of three family
clans—the Wolf, the Turtle,
or the Turkey. Each clan

17

Delaware babies belonged to the mother's clan.

was related to the larger world through their mother's link with that animal's spirit. The spirit of each animal helped members of its clan. The Wolf also was concerned with the land, the Turtle with the water, and the Turkey with the sky.

Every longhouse had a picture of a Wolf, Turtle, or Turkey over the doors so people would know who lived there.

All the women in a longhouse belonged to the

Grandmothers, mothers, and daughters lived in the same house.

same clan. Grandmothers, mothers, sisters, and daughters lived together.

A husband moved into the longhouse of his wife's clan. His wife had to belong to another clan. If a Wolf clan man married a Turtle clan woman, for example, their children belonged to the Turtle clan.

Children belonged with their mother. Their father was not considered a close relative. Instead, their mother's brothers took care of the children's training and education. A father took care of his sister's

children, but not his own.
Little boys had a tattoo
of their mother's clan animal
on their chest so that
if they got lost, people knew
where to take them.

Most of the longhouses
in a town belonged to the
same clan. Since the clan
owned the land where its
people hunted and farmed,
members of a clan stayed
together.

Every clan had two men
to lead it. One was the

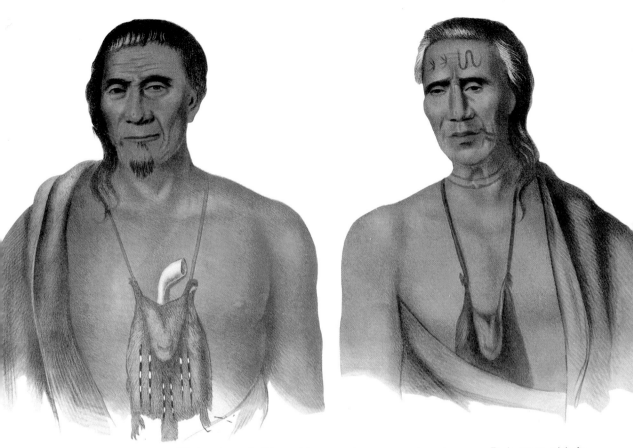

Tishcohan (left) and Lappawinze were two famous Delaware chiefs.

clan chief, who made sure
that everything ran
smoothly in the community.
The other was the clan
captain, who led in times
of war.

These men were leaders only as long as they behaved well. If they did wrong or hurt people, then the women of the clan—their mothers and sisters—took the job away from them and gave it to someone who could do better.

Although Delaware women did not speak in public or hold office as men did, they had the final say in how a clan was managed.

Left: A Delaware man and his two sisters. Women picked the leaders for the clan. Above: Drawing of a Delaware carving of a spirit called a manitou.

VISIONS

Before their voices changed, boys were taught to fast. They learned how to pray to earn the goodwill of one of the many spirits who lived on the earth or in the sky.

The Delaware believed these spirits gave the boys the power to work hard, gain respect, and be a success. Girls sometimes fasted and prayed, too.

Every kind of work required the help of a spirit. The spirit appeared in a vision and taught the child a special song. Every time the child sang that song, the spirit came to help.

The most important job requiring spiritual help was

Delaware doctors danced and prayed during a cure.

that of the doctor. The
Delaware had several
kinds of doctors, both men
and women. They used
herbs and medicines to
cure the sick. Sometimes,
the doctor used a sweat
lodge to treat the patient.
In the most serious cases,
doctors used their special

27

healing powers
to make
someone well.
    Once a
Delaware had
a vision and a
spirit guardian,
he or she could
marry and
start a family.

A Delaware family

RITUALS

Important families led their clan in rituals every year to give thanks for nature's bounty.

Two ceremonies were especially important in Delaware religion—the Corn Dance and the Big House ceremony.

Every fall when the corn was ripe, a big dance was held to thank the

Native Americans raised corn varieties of many different colors.

Corn Mother for allowing the crop to be harvested.

The grandest ceremony of all was called the Big House. In every large town, a community center was built. It had bark shingles and a peaked roof.

The peak was held up by a long pole that rested on a carved post. On either side of this center post, faces were carved to represent the Creator. Half of his face was painted black, and the other half red. This tall post represented the cedar tree in the beginning of the world.

The oval-shaped floor around the post represented the back of the turtle that held up the world. This was a model of the world as the Delaware knew it.

For twelve days, people gathered in the town and worshiped in the Big House. Each night, every man who had a vision sang and danced to tell about the spirit he had met. At dawn, the songs ended and everyone ate. The people rested during the day, but no one slept. They were there to worship and thank the Creator.

Children wearing Delaware dress at a powwow in Oklahoma. At a powwow, Native Americans get together to celebrate their traditions.

On the last night, everyone dressed in their best clothes. Women who had visions and some young men from good families sang and danced.

33

On the last morning, everyone went out of the Big House in single file. They stood in a line and said a loud prayer asking the Creator for another year of life.

The Delaware had a life that was hard but happy. They had to work all the time to stay fed and clothed, but everyone in the family helped and had fun together.

Landing of the Swedish colonists at Paradise Point, in the Delaware homeland

CHANGES

After the Europeans came, everything changed. Spanish, French, Dutch, and English colonists fought over the land and what they could take from it.

Sweden sent colonists to settle among the southern

Delaware. The Swedes demanded food and land, but they were so few in number that they did not fight the Delaware.

Then the Dutch took over and many people were killed in wars.

The English took over from the Dutch, and they wanted land for settlers. The Delaware were forced to sign treaties giving up their lands. This made the Delaware sad and confused. For as long as

At first, the Quaker colonists got along well with the Native Americans. This painting shows William Penn's treaty with the Delaware.

they could, they sold only bits and pieces of their lands.

The Quakers, sent by William Penn, settled in Pennsylvania and enjoyed good relations with the

Delaware. Things turned bad, however, when Penn's sons needed money. They cheated the Delaware out of their land and sold it for a profit.

The Delaware had to leave their homeland and move west. Many people were sick and unhappy.

The Delaware tried to make a new home in several states, but they were always driven away. First, they moved to Ohio. There, they took part in

the American Revolution.
Some fought for the British
and some for the
Americans, but most tried
to stay neutral.

In Ohio, in 1782, an
entire town of Christian
Delaware was killed by
American soldiers. The

A drawing
showing the
killing of the
Christian
Delaware in Ohio.

Soldiers of the American Revolution destroyed Delaware villages in Ohio.

other Delaware were very sad to lose so many relatives.

From Ohio, many Delaware went into Canada, where their descendants still live today. The rest of the Delaware moved to Indiana. There, a woman prophet preached to them. At that time, many Native American prophets were teaching a new and better way to live during hostile times. Only the Delaware had a prophet who was a woman. They listened to her carefully.

Soon, the Delaware lived better and started to help each other. But then they were forced to move again.

They went to Missouri and then to Kansas, where

Delaware families finally
found a home in Oklahoma, where
they started farms and ranches.

they were happy until
wagon trains and soldiers
again pushed them off
their lands.

So they moved again.
This time they joined many
42 other tribes who came to

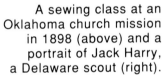
A sewing class at an
Oklahoma church mission
in 1898 (above) and a
portrait of Jack Harry,
a Delaware scout (right).

Indian Territory. By 1869,
the Delaware at last had
a home they could call
their own. When Indian
Territory became the state
of Oklahoma, the
Delaware remained.

Today, the Delaware people work in modern businesses and industries. Alexis Nicole Parton (left), is shown with her father at her college graduation. Mary Christine Johnson Spybuck (right) was a member of the Delaware council.

Today, just like other men in Oklahoma, Delaware fathers work in oil fields, stores, offices, and factories. The mothers work at home and in

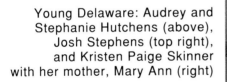

Young Delaware: Audrey and
Stephanie Hutchens (above),
Josh Stephens (top right),
and Kristen Paige Skinner
with her mother, Mary Ann (right)

offices. Delaware children
go to school just like other
children, but they know
that their traditions were a
special gift to their nation
from the Creator.

45

WORDS YOU SHOULD KNOW

ceremony (SAIR • ih • moh • nee)—a celebration or a religious service

colonist (KAHL • uh • nist)—a person who goes to another country to live and work

community (kuh • MYOO • nih • tee)—a group of people who live close together

compartment (kum • PART • mint)—one of the parts into which a space is divided by walls

fast (FAST)—to go without food

goodwill (good • WIL)—a feeling of friendliness

guardian (GAR • dee • yun)—one who watches over a person and keeps that person from harm

herbs (ERBZ)—plants whose leaves or roots can be used for medicines

neutral (NOO • tril)—not favoring one side or the other

prophet (PRAH • fit)—a person who gives spiritual messages or warnings or foretells the future

reverence (REV • er • ins)—a feeling of respect for the spirits

ritual (RIT • choo • il)—a special set of actions used in religious ceremonies

settlers (SET • lerz)—people who come to a new country to establish farms and other homes

sweat lodge (SWET LAHJ)—a hut heated by steam from water poured on hot stones—used by Native Americans

traditions (truh • DISH • unz)—ancient customs and beliefs

treaty (TREE • tee)—a written agreement between two groups having to do with trade, peace, land rights, law, etc.

tribe (TRYBE)—a group of people related by blood and customs

vision (VIZH • un)—a dream-like visit from a spirit

INDEX

About the Author

Jay Miller lives in Seattle so he can eat salmon and visit the nearby reservations, mountains, streams, and ocean. He enjoys hiking in the mountains, kayaking, and eating pie as much he enjoys being a writer, professor, and lecturer. His family is complex but delightful. He belongs to the Delaware Wolf clan.

He went to college at the University of New Mexico and Rutgers University. He also learned from elders all over the Americas, who taught him the best stuff of all.

For help in reading and writing these books, he wants to thank Vi, Noah, Zachary, and Sara. Rebecca, Keri, Megan, Garrett, Erica, and Aaron also helped in their own ways.

This book is dedicated to the honor and memory of Nora Thompson Dean and Lucy Parks Blalock.